Oskar & Klaus

coloring book

PROJECT ADVISOR: **MICK SZYDLOWSKI**

COVER ART BY: **MANUEL PREITANO**

ARTWORK BY: **MANUEL PREITANO**

PROJECT MANAGER: **Grant Alter**

BOOK DESIGN BY: **Les Dabel**

www.glasshousegraphics.com

FOLLOW US ONLINE:
WWW.DABELBROTHERS.COM

Twitter: @DabelBrothers
Facebook: facebook.com/dabelbrothers

DONATE TO CATS IN NEED
www.milossanctuary.org/donate

DABEL BROTHERS:

Jay Gentry - CEO
Ernst Dabel - President
Les Dabel - V.P. Licensing
Derek Ruiz - Publisher
Patrick Victor - V.P. Sales

Grant Alter - Editor-in-Chief
Dave Lanphear - Chief Creative Officer
Gladys Atwell - Marketing Director
Anthony Zicari: - Editor / Sr. Writer

Helen Keller once wrote that "life is either a daring adventure or nothing." The spirit of her words is captured perfectly by a blind cat named Oskar, who was born with an insatiable urge to explore his world, frequently with his reluctant sidekick, Klaus. Their humble roots — Oskar started life as a Midwestern farm kitten and Klaus a stray— don't hold them back from living life to the fullest. Won't you join them for at least a few of their giant, epic adventures in the remote corners of the globe? One thing is certain: you will quickly discover that there's no limit to what a blind cat can do!

Thanks again!

Mick

Tips on how to color this Coloring Book:

Thank you for purchasing this Dabel Brothers Coloring Book.

It's one of many Coloring Books we currently have available from your favorite authors, book series, TV shows, Movies, Games, Musician... the list goes on and will continue to grow as we add more amazing Coloring Books to our lineup.

If you enjoyed this Coloring Book please make sure to post your colored pages on our social media and leave us a review. We also encourage you to purchase a copy for your loved ones, as coloring is a great source of stress relief.

Make sure to visit our website DabelBrothers.com for news on upcoming titles and free goodies.

Yours Truly,

Dabel Brothers

1 Always test any markers before you start coloring, using the test page in the back of the book to see if the marker bleeds through or leaves a shadow.

2 If you are using a marker, paint or watercolor pencils. Slip a piece of paper behind the page your are coloring to protect the pages behind from bleed through issues.

3 Have LOTS of fun coloring and always remember, coloring is twice as fun when you are coloring with others. So make sure you have plenty of copies of this book for you and your loved ones :)

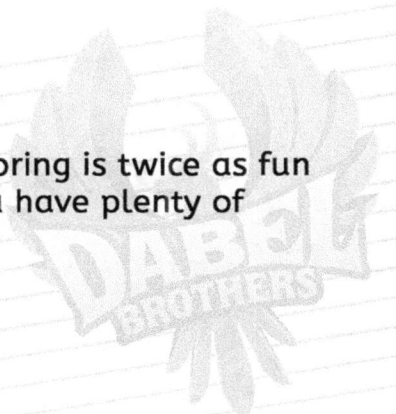

As some of the first cats to visit space, Oskar and Klaus made absolutely sure their ship was well stocked with their favorite space food.

In their beloved Vespaw, Oskar and Klaus went on a whirlwind drive across Europe. This is from their visit to Italy.

Oskar and Klaus - Totally radical kittie skaters.

Oskar and Klaus rock out at Budokat. All the fans go nuts!

Oskar and Klaus go scuba diving looking to make new, exotic fishy friends. Looks like that shark wants to play.

Oskar may not be able to see, but he sure loves flying in a biplane.

Öskar&Klaus

"I told you a dinosaur park didn't 'sound like fun!' Why don't you ever listen?"

From up in their hot air balloon, Klaus can see everything. He describes what he sees in vivid detail to Oskar, who loves feeling the breeze on his whiskers.

"I'm not sure this crocodile is the right one to ask for directions."

Oskar tells Klaus about his dream where they visited the great Sphinx, but he was a bit off on proportions.

Oskar and Klaus on safari.

"Trust me, it's a massive UFO, it's right behind us, and we better RUN FAST!"

Oskar and Klaus pose for the cover of their very first coloring book.

Oskar and Klaus love Japan.

"Step on my tail again and you just might
get the paw, even in front of a crowd!"

"ARRRRRRR-AWWK! We've got you now, Oskar and Klaus!"

"We love Paris. What architecture!"

Oskar and Klaus are looking to eat seafood, not become seafood!

"Cut! I said a pan, not a close-up!"

Oskar and Klaus: buddies for life.

Test Page: